Cryptocurrency 101

A Beginner's Guide to Bitcoin, Ethereum, Blockchain, and Digital Currency Basics

By Joe Correa

Published by Live Stronger Faster

This book is for educational and informational purposes only. The author and publisher are not engaged in rendering legal, financial, or other professional advice. Readers should consult a qualified professional before making any financial decisions.

First Edition

Table of Contents

Introduction

Welcome to *Cryptocurrency 101*, the first book in the *Crypto Wealth Academy* series. If you're holding this book, chances are you've either heard about Bitcoin, Ethereum, or perhaps you've seen stories of everyday people turning small investments into life-changing wealth — and you're wondering what it all means and how to be part of it. You're in the right place. This book was created to be your clear, non-technical, and practical guide to understanding the foundations of cryptocurrency — without needing a background in finance or computer science.

Cryptocurrency isn't just about "making money fast" or jumping on a digital trend. It represents a shift — a fundamental transformation in how money, trust, value, and ownership work in the digital era. Just like the internet changed communication forever, blockchain technology and cryptocurrency are changing how we store value, perform transactions, and build wealth. But with all the noise, scams, hype, and tech jargon out there, it's easy to feel overwhelmed or intimidated. That's why this book breaks it all down from the beginning.

We'll start by answering the most basic — yet most important — questions: What is cryptocurrency? What is blockchain?

How does Bitcoin work? Why does Ethereum matter? What makes this system different from the traditional banking system? And how can an ordinary person begin using and investing in this new digital economy safely and wisely?

Whether your goal is to invest a few hundred dollars, build a full-time crypto income, or simply understand what your kids or coworkers are talking about, this book is the perfect launchpad. You'll learn how digital wallets work, what mining means, the differences between tokens and coins, how to buy and store crypto securely, and most importantly — how to avoid common beginner mistakes that lead to lost money or scams. You'll also gain context around the history of money, the failures of centralized finance, and how blockchain is solving real-world problems globally.

But this isn't just about knowledge. The *Crypto Wealth Academy* series is about transformation. It's about equipping you to take action and build lasting digital wealth in the same way people learned to invest in stocks or real estate in previous generations. Only now, the rules are different, and the opportunities are much faster-moving. We're entering a future where decentralized finance, tokenized assets, smart contracts, and borderless money are becoming the norm — and those who understand these tools early are the ones who will benefit the most.

Each chapter of this book builds your confidence layer by layer. By the end of *Cryptocurrency 101*, you'll not only understand the basics but also be able to explain them to someone else. You'll feel prepared to take your first steps in buying, storing, and securing cryptocurrency. Most importantly, you'll be ready to move on to the next books in this series, where we go deeper into investing strategies, passive income opportunities, DeFi platforms, NFTs, crypto taxes, advanced trading, and even creating your own crypto projects.

I've designed this series to follow a natural learning path — from absolute beginner to advanced user — and to keep everything practical, real-world, and easy to follow. I've worked with new crypto users from all walks of life, and I know the exact roadblocks people face. That's why we keep the jargon minimal and focus on clarity and results. This is not just theory — it's real knowledge you can apply today, wherever you are in the world.

So get ready. Whether you're completely new to cryptocurrency or just need a refresher, this first book will set the stage for your journey toward digital financial freedom. Take notes, pause and reflect, revisit key sections as needed, and most of all — take action. The future of money isn't coming — it's already here. The only question is whether you'll watch from the sidelines or step into the game. Let's begin.

Chapter 1: What is Cryptocurrency and Why Does It Matter?

Cryptocurrency is a type of digital currency that uses cryptography — a form of advanced mathematics and coding — to secure transactions, control the creation of new units, and verify the transfer of assets on a decentralized network. Unlike traditional currencies such as the U.S. dollar or the euro, cryptocurrency is not issued by any government or central authority. Instead, it operates on a peer-to-peer network, meaning transactions happen directly between users without the need for a bank or intermediary. This is made possible through blockchain technology, which is the foundation of all cryptocurrencies.

A blockchain is a distributed ledger — essentially a shared database — that records all transactions in chronological order. The unique thing about this ledger is that it is maintained across a network of computers called nodes, and every participant has a copy of it. Once a transaction is added to the blockchain, it is nearly impossible to change or remove. This makes it extremely secure and transparent, which is one of the key reasons cryptocurrency has gained such a following. No single person or organization controls the blockchain, which makes it resistant to censorship, fraud, and government interference.

Bitcoin, the first and most well-known cryptocurrency, was created in 2009 by an unknown individual or group using the pseudonym Satoshi Nakamoto. It was introduced in response to the 2008 global financial crisis as a way to create a currency that could not be manipulated by banks or governments. Bitcoin allows people to send value across the internet without relying on trust in a central authority. Since then, thousands of other cryptocurrencies have been created, each with its own features, purposes, and communities. Ethereum, for example, introduced smart contracts — self-executing agreements that automatically carry out actions when conditions are met — opening the door for decentralized applications (DApps) that can run without downtime or human interference.

The appeal of cryptocurrency lies in its unique advantages over traditional money. First, it is borderless. You can send cryptocurrency to anyone, anywhere in the world, in a matter of minutes without worrying about currency conversion, banking hours, or international transfer fees. Second, it provides financial inclusion. Millions of people around the world do not have access to a bank account but can own and use cryptocurrency simply with a smartphone and internet connection. Third, it offers transparency and security through blockchain technology. All transactions are recorded publicly, yet personal identities remain private through the use of digital wallet addresses.

However, it's important to understand that cryptocurrency is not without risks. Prices can be extremely volatile, often swinging dramatically within hours or days. This volatility can lead to both significant gains and devastating losses. Additionally, the crypto space is still relatively new and largely unregulated in many countries, making it a target for scams, hacks, and fraudulent projects. Without proper education and caution, beginners can easily lose their funds by sending them to the wrong address, investing in a fake project, or failing to secure their private keys.

Understanding how cryptocurrency works is the first step toward using it effectively. At its core, cryptocurrency transactions are verified by a network of computers using consensus mechanisms. Bitcoin, for example, uses proof-of-work, where miners solve complex mathematical puzzles to validate transactions and earn rewards. Ethereum is transitioning to proof-of-stake, where validators are chosen based on the amount of cryptocurrency they hold and are willing to "stake" as collateral. These systems ensure that the network operates smoothly and fairly without relying on a central authority.

For anyone looking to get started, the key is to begin small and focus on learning before risking significant amounts of money. This means setting up a secure digital wallet, understanding the difference between hot wallets (connected to the internet) and cold wallets (offline storage), and learning how to buy, sell, and store cryptocurrency safely. It also means staying up to date on news, regulations, and technological advancements in the space. The world of cryptocurrency is fast-moving, and what is true today may be outdated in a few months.

In summary, cryptocurrency matters because it represents a shift in how we think about money, ownership, and trust. It empowers individuals to control their wealth without relying on banks, opens financial opportunities to people excluded from the traditional system, and offers a transparent and secure way to store and transfer value. At the same time, it requires personal responsibility, as there is no customer service line to call if you make a mistake. If you approach it with curiosity, caution, and the right knowledge, cryptocurrency can be a powerful tool for building wealth in the digital age.

Let's go over an interesting story now.

In a small town on the outskirts of Lisbon, a young woman named Sofia sat in a crowded café, her laptop open and a steaming espresso by her side. She was 27 years old, working as a freelance graphic designer, and although her income was steady, she always felt the invisible weight of financial insecurity. One evening, a client from Singapore offered to pay her in something called "Bitcoin." At the time, she had no idea what it was, but curiosity got the better of her. She researched late into the night, reading articles and watching videos, trying to understand why anyone would use a digital coin instead of regular money.

Her first discovery was the concept of decentralization — the idea that no government or bank controlled Bitcoin. This fascinated her, especially after hearing stories of friends back in her hometown who lost their savings when their country's banks froze accounts during an economic crisis. She thought, *If my money isn't in a bank, can anyone really take it from me?* That thought alone was enough to keep her reading. She learned about blockchain, a digital ledger that anyone could see but no one could tamper with. It sounded almost magical — a system that ran on pure math and community trust instead of politics.

The next day, Sofia downloaded a mobile wallet app and sent her first request for payment in Bitcoin. Minutes later, the payment arrived, and she watched in awe as the transaction appeared on her screen, confirmed by the network. There were no delays, no conversion fees, and no bank clerks asking invasive questions. She suddenly understood that this was more than money — it was freedom. Over the next few weeks, she continued experimenting, buying a small amount of Ethereum, learning about smart contracts, and even trying her hand at a decentralized exchange. Each step pulled her deeper into the world of cryptocurrency, where every new concept seemed to unlock another possibility.

But Sofia also learned the hard way that with great power came great responsibility. One afternoon, she sent a small test payment to what she thought was a friend's wallet address. A single digit was off. The funds disappeared instantly, and there was no way to reverse the transaction. The mistake cost her $50 — not a fortune, but enough to teach her a lesson she would never forget. From then on, she triple-checked every address, kept backups of her private keys, and started storing most of her crypto in a cold wallet for added safety.

Months later, Sofia found herself speaking confidently about cryptocurrency to friends who had once dismissed it as a fad. She explained how it could help people in unstable economies protect their savings, how it allowed freelancers like her to work for clients anywhere in the world without worrying about banks, and how it opened doors to investments once reserved for the wealthy. She wasn't a millionaire — not yet — but she had something just as valuable: control over her own financial destiny. For the first time in her life, she felt she was playing a game where the rules weren't stacked against her.

Sofia's story is not unique. Around the world, millions of people are discovering cryptocurrency for the first time, driven by curiosity, necessity, or the desire for independence. Some will make fortunes, others will make mistakes, but all will be part of a global shift in how we think about and use money. For Sofia, Bitcoin was more than a payment option — it was the key to a future where she was in charge. And that's why cryptocurrency matters.

Chapter 2: The History and Evolution of Money

Money is one of humanity's oldest inventions, and understanding its history helps explain why cryptocurrency exists today. Long before digital wallets and blockchain, early civilizations relied on bartering — directly exchanging goods and services without a standardized medium of exchange. A farmer might trade grain for a fisherman's catch, or a potter might swap clay bowls for animal hides. While bartering worked in small communities, it had clear limitations: what if the fisherman didn't need grain that day? This problem, known as the "coincidence of wants," led to the creation of money.

The earliest forms of money were commodity-based. Societies used items like salt, livestock, cowrie shells, and even large stones to represent value. These items were chosen because they were scarce, durable, and widely accepted. Eventually, precious metals like gold and silver became the dominant form of money because they were portable, divisible, and could be standardized into coins. These metals also had intrinsic value — they were useful beyond their role as money, which helped people trust them.

As trade expanded and economies grew, carrying large amounts of metal became impractical. This led to the birth of paper money, first in China during the Tang Dynasty and later in Europe. Paper currency was initially backed by precious metals, meaning you could exchange it for gold or silver upon request. This system, known as the gold standard, provided stability and trust because the money's value was tied to a tangible asset. However, over time, governments realized they could issue more paper currency than the gold they had, which allowed them to finance wars and large projects but also caused inflation.

In the 20th century, most countries abandoned the gold standard entirely, moving to fiat currency. Fiat money has value because a government declares it legal tender and people trust that others will accept it in exchange for goods and services. It is no longer backed by physical commodities but instead by the stability and credit of the issuing government. This shift allowed for greater economic flexibility but also opened the door to problems like inflation, currency devaluation, and overreliance on central banks.

Technological progress brought about the next stage in money's evolution — electronic payments. Credit cards, online banking, and payment processors like PayPal made it easier than ever to send money around the world. However, these systems still relied on centralized intermediaries that could freeze accounts, charge high fees, and limit access for certain individuals or countries. The 2008 global financial crisis exposed just how fragile and flawed the traditional system could be, with banks failing, currencies collapsing, and ordinary people losing their savings.

It was in this climate of distrust and instability that Bitcoin emerged in 2009. Unlike fiat money, Bitcoin was not issued by any central authority. Its value came from its scarcity (only 21 million coins will ever exist), its security through blockchain technology, and the trust of the people using it. This was a radical departure from thousands of years of centralized money management. In many ways, cryptocurrency is a return to the principles that made gold valuable: scarcity, durability, and independence from political control — but updated for the digital age.

The transition from barter to crypto represents humanity's ongoing quest for more efficient, secure, and fair systems of exchange. Each stage in this evolution addressed the shortcomings of the one before it, but also introduced new challenges. Cryptocurrency is simply the latest chapter in this story — and perhaps the first form of money truly suited to a borderless, internet-connected world. Understanding how money has evolved prepares you to appreciate the revolutionary nature of digital currencies and why they may play a central role in the future of global finance.

Karim's story

In the bustling marketplace of Marrakech, a merchant named Karim stood behind his stall of spices, his hands stained with saffron and turmeric. He had inherited the business from his father, who had inherited it from his grandfather. For generations, the family had sold their goods in exchange for gold coins, silver dirhams, or — in leaner times — whatever their customers could trade. Karim's earliest memory of business was weighing saffron on a brass scale and watching a traveler from Europe hand his father a small gold coin in return.

One afternoon, a tourist approached his stall and pulled out a thin, colorful banknote instead of gold. Karim hesitated. He had heard of paper money but never held it before. The note was light, almost flimsy compared to the reassuring weight of gold, but the man explained that it could be exchanged at the local bank for coins or other goods. Reluctantly, Karim accepted it. Over time, paper money became more common, and Karim found himself counting stacks of notes instead of coins. It was easier to carry but also easier to lose — one gust of wind, and a day's earnings could scatter down the street.

Years later, his son Jamal took over the stall. By then, credit card machines had appeared in the marketplace. Jamal could sell saffron to someone without a single coin or note changing hands. The bank would deposit the funds directly into his account — minus a fee, of course. Business was good, but Jamal noticed something troubling: if the bank decided to freeze his account, he would have no way to access his money. He heard stories of friends whose accounts were closed without warning, leaving them stranded.

Then came the global financial crisis. Prices soared, tourists dwindled, and the local currency lost value almost overnight. Jamal's savings could buy less and less each month. One evening, his nephew, who was studying abroad, called to tell him about something called Bitcoin — a type of money that no government controlled. Intrigued, Jamal asked how it worked. His nephew explained blockchain technology, digital wallets, and the idea of a currency that could be sent anywhere in the world instantly, without banks.

Skeptical but curious, Jamal decided to accept Bitcoin for a small sale to a tech-savvy tourist. The payment arrived on his phone in minutes, confirmed by a string of numbers and letters instead of a bank receipt. A week later, the value of that Bitcoin had increased. Jamal realized that this was more than just a way to get paid — it was a way to store value that no bank could seize and no government could devalue at will.

As he closed his stall one evening, Jamal thought about his grandfather trading spices for gold, his father adapting to paper money, and his own shift to digital payments. Each generation had faced the same challenge: learning to trust a new kind of money. Now it was his turn. Bitcoin, he thought, was simply the next step in a journey humanity had been on for thousands of years — but this time, he had a chance to get in early.

Chapter 3: Understanding Blockchain Technology

Blockchain is the backbone of cryptocurrency — the technology that makes it possible for digital currencies like Bitcoin and Ethereum to function securely without the need for a central authority. At its simplest, a blockchain is a digital ledger, a record-keeping system that stores data in a series of linked blocks. These blocks contain information about transactions and are connected in chronological order, forming a "chain" that is publicly visible and permanent.

The term "blockchain" comes from the way this ledger is structured. Each block contains three main components: the transaction data, a timestamp, and a cryptographic hash (a unique fingerprint) of the block. It also stores the hash of the previous block, creating a continuous and unbreakable chain. This design ensures that if someone were to try altering the data in a single block, the hash would change, breaking the link and immediately alerting the network to potential tampering.

One of the key strengths of blockchain is decentralization. Instead of being stored on a single server or controlled by a single institution, blockchain data is distributed across thousands — or even millions — of computers around the world, known as nodes. Every node has a copy of the blockchain, and all copies are constantly synchronized through a consensus mechanism. This means that no single point of failure exists, making the system extremely resistant to hacking, censorship, or data loss.

Consensus mechanisms are how blockchain networks agree on the validity of transactions. The two most common are proof-of-work (PoW) and proof-of-stake (PoS). In PoW, miners compete to solve complex mathematical puzzles, and the first to solve it gets to add the next block to the chain and receive a reward. This method, used by Bitcoin, is secure but energy-intensive. PoS, used by Ethereum after its 2022 upgrade, selects validators based on the amount of cryptocurrency they have staked as collateral. This method uses far less energy and allows for faster transaction processing.

Another important feature of blockchain is transparency combined with privacy. Every transaction is recorded publicly, and anyone can view it, but the identities of the people involved are hidden behind cryptographic wallet addresses. This balance allows for accountability without revealing personal details, which is especially important for global financial systems.

Blockchain's applications extend far beyond cryptocurrency. It can be used for supply chain tracking, voting systems, medical record storage, identity verification, and even real estate transactions. The technology's ability to create trust in a trustless environment — where parties do not need to know or rely on each other — opens up new possibilities for commerce and governance.

Security is built into the blockchain's structure. Because each block is linked to the one before it through cryptographic hashes, altering one block would require altering every subsequent block across the entire network — a task that is virtually impossible for large, well-established blockchains. This immutability makes blockchain a reliable way to store critical data.

For a cryptocurrency investor or user, understanding blockchain is essential because it explains why cryptocurrencies are different from traditional digital payment systems like PayPal or bank transfers. In traditional systems, a central authority verifies and processes transactions, while in blockchain, the network of nodes collectively validates them. This decentralization not only prevents fraud but also gives individuals full control over their assets.

In essence, blockchain is not just a financial tool — it's a foundational technology for the future of digital transactions. By enabling secure, decentralized, and transparent systems, blockchain lays the groundwork for a world where trust is embedded in the code, not in intermediaries. Once you grasp how blockchain works, you can better appreciate why cryptocurrencies have the potential to reshape industries far beyond finance.

Ji-ho becomes a blockchain explorer

On a rainy afternoon in Seoul, a young software engineer named Ji-ho sat in his apartment, staring at the glowing code on his laptop. He had been fascinated by technology since childhood, but blockchain was something entirely new. A friend had once told him, "It's like a bank ledger, but no one owns it." That sounded impossible. How could something be secure if no one was in charge?

Curious, Ji-ho joined an online community of blockchain enthusiasts. They explained that instead of trusting one bank to record transactions, a blockchain lets thousands of computers around the world keep identical copies of the same ledger. If one tried to cheat, the others would immediately reject it. The system was built on mathematics, not personal trust. Ji-ho compared it to a game where every player kept their own scorecard, and they all checked each other's math after every move.

Determined to see it in action, Ji-ho downloaded a blockchain explorer and began tracing Bitcoin transactions. He was amazed to see payments from Brazil to Germany, from Canada to Kenya — all confirmed within minutes, without banks or governments approving them. He realized that this wasn't just about sending money; it was about creating a global network where anyone could transact with anyone else directly.

His fascination deepened when he learned about smart contracts on the Ethereum blockchain. The idea that computer code could automatically execute agreements without lawyers or middlemen felt revolutionary. He imagined buying a house where the deed transferred instantly once payment was made, or voting in an election where results were verified instantly and transparently.

One night, while working late, Ji-ho received a message from a nonprofit in Africa. They had read one of his blog posts about blockchain and wanted his help to track food shipments using the technology. In countries where corruption had siphoned off aid for decades, blockchain could ensure that every bag of rice reached its intended destination. Ji-ho agreed, and within months, the system was in place. Donors could see exactly when and where their contributions arrived, and fraud dropped dramatically.

The project changed Ji-ho's perspective. Blockchain was not just a tool for trading cryptocurrency — it was a way to build trust in places where trust had been broken. He realized that while most people were drawn to crypto for its potential profits, the real power of blockchain lay in its ability to create fairness and accountability on a global scale.

Years later, Ji-ho still held some Bitcoin and Ethereum, but his pride came from the systems he built that improved people's lives. To him, blockchain was like the internet in its early days — a vast, untapped frontier with possibilities far beyond what most people could imagine. And he knew he was lucky to have been one of the early explorers.

Chapter 4: How Bitcoin Works

Bitcoin is the first and most recognized cryptocurrency in the world, and understanding how it works is essential for anyone entering the crypto space. At its core, Bitcoin is a decentralized digital currency that allows peer-to-peer transactions over the internet without relying on banks or payment processors. It was introduced in 2009 by an anonymous creator known as Satoshi Nakamoto, whose goal was to create "a purely peer-to-peer version of electronic cash" that could operate without the need for trust in a central authority.

Bitcoin operates on a public blockchain — a shared ledger that records every transaction ever made on the network. Each transaction is grouped into a block, and each block is linked to the one before it through cryptographic hashes, forming an immutable chain. This blockchain is maintained by thousands of computers worldwide called nodes, which all have a copy of the ledger and verify new transactions through a process called mining.

Mining is the process by which Bitcoin transactions are validated and added to the blockchain. Miners use powerful computers to solve complex mathematical puzzles in a system called proof-of-work (PoW). The first miner to solve the puzzle gets to add the new block of transactions to the blockchain and is rewarded with newly created bitcoins plus transaction fees. This process not only secures the network but also controls the creation of new bitcoins, which are introduced at a fixed and predictable rate.

One of Bitcoin's most important features is its limited supply. There will only ever be 21 million bitcoins in existence, and this scarcity is one reason Bitcoin is often referred to as "digital gold." New bitcoins are released through mining rewards, which are cut in half approximately every four years in an event called the "halving." This gradual reduction in supply, combined with increasing demand, has contributed to Bitcoin's significant price appreciation over time.

Transactions in Bitcoin are secured using public-key cryptography. Each user has a pair of cryptographic keys: a public key, which acts like an address where funds can be sent, and a private key, which must be kept secret because it allows you to spend your bitcoins. If you lose your private key, you lose access to your funds permanently — there is no "forgot password" option in Bitcoin. This personal responsibility is both a strength and a challenge of using the currency.

Bitcoin transactions are pseudonymous, meaning that while wallet addresses are visible on the blockchain, they are not directly linked to your personal identity unless you choose to reveal it. This offers privacy but also makes Bitcoin attractive to criminals, which has led to debates about regulation. In many countries, cryptocurrency exchanges are now required to follow know-your-customer (KYC) and anti-money-laundering (AML) laws, requiring users to verify their identities before trading.

The Bitcoin network is designed to be resilient. Because it is decentralized, there is no single point of failure that can be shut down by governments or hackers. Even if part of the network goes offline, the rest can continue processing transactions. This resilience has allowed Bitcoin to survive multiple attempts at banning or regulating it out of existence.

For investors, Bitcoin is seen as both a store of value and a potential hedge against inflation, similar to gold. Its price can be volatile in the short term, but its long-term trend has historically been upward, attracting both retail investors and large institutions. Whether you view it as an alternative currency, a speculative asset, or a long-term investment, understanding how Bitcoin works is the first step toward using it effectively.

The story of how Carlos bought his first Bitcoin

In Buenos Aires, inflation was eating away at people's savings faster than they could earn. Carlos, a 35-year-old accountant, had watched his purchasing power shrink year after year. He remembered when his parents lost nearly everything during the economic crisis of the early 2000s, and now history seemed to be repeating itself. No matter how much he worked, his bank balance was worth less every month.

One evening, over coffee with a friend, Carlos heard about Bitcoin. His friend described it as "money that no government can print more of." Intrigued, Carlos went home and began reading about it. He learned that Bitcoin was limited to 21 million coins, that it was stored on a public blockchain, and that it could be sent anywhere in the world without needing a bank. The idea of controlling his money without trusting a government or financial institution was both thrilling and unnerving.

Carlos decided to start small. He signed up for a cryptocurrency exchange, completed the identity verification, and bought a fraction of a Bitcoin — just enough to experiment. At first, it felt strange seeing a number like 0.005 BTC in his account instead of pesos or dollars. But when he transferred it to his mobile wallet and saw the transaction confirm in minutes, he realized he had just moved value across the internet without asking anyone for permission.

As the months passed, Carlos began to see Bitcoin as more than an investment — it was a lifeline. When the peso dropped sharply, the value of his Bitcoin, despite its volatility, held far better than his savings account. He began accepting Bitcoin as payment from a few clients, storing part of his earnings in a hardware wallet that he kept hidden at home. He learned to back up his private keys and triple-check wallet addresses before sending transactions. The sense of control was empowering.

One day, Carlos's cousin in Spain needed money urgently. In the past, international transfers would have taken days and cost a small fortune in fees. This time, Carlos sent her Bitcoin, and she received it in under 10 minutes. The entire process cost less than a dollar in transaction fees. For Carlos, this was a turning point. Bitcoin wasn't just an asset — it was a faster, fairer way to move money globally.

Over time, Carlos became the "Bitcoin guy" in his social circle, teaching friends how to set up wallets, secure their private keys, and avoid scams. He warned them that Bitcoin prices could swing wildly and that it wasn't a get-rich-quick scheme. But he also shared his belief that Bitcoin was the most important financial invention of his lifetime — a tool that could give people power over their own money in a way that no bank or government ever had.

As Argentina's economy continued to struggle, Carlos's decision to learn about Bitcoin gave him not just financial stability, but also hope. He knew the road ahead would have risks, but he also knew he had stepped into a new world where, for the first time, the rules of money were not dictated by politicians or central bankers — but by code, mathematics, and a network of people who believed in something better.

Chapter 5: How Ethereum Works and the Power of Smart Contracts

Ethereum is the second-largest cryptocurrency by market capitalization, but it is far more than just "another Bitcoin." While Bitcoin was designed primarily as a peer-to-peer digital currency and store of value, Ethereum was built as a platform for decentralized applications (DApps) powered by *smart contracts*. These smart contracts are self-executing programs that run exactly as coded, without the need for intermediaries, downtime, or censorship.

Launched in 2015 by programmer Vitalik Buterin and a team of co-founders, Ethereum introduced a blockchain that could do much more than record simple transactions. Instead of just sending value from one person to another, Ethereum's blockchain can execute complex programs that automate agreements, manage digital assets, or even create entirely new cryptocurrencies. This innovation opened the door to a wide range of use cases, from decentralized finance (DeFi) to non-fungible tokens (NFTs), gaming economies, supply chain tracking, and beyond.

At the heart of Ethereum's ecosystem is its native cryptocurrency, Ether (ETH). While Ether can be used like Bitcoin for peer-to-peer transactions, its primary role is to fuel the Ethereum network. When you execute a transaction or run a smart contract, you must pay a fee called "gas," which is paid in Ether. Gas fees compensate the network's validators for processing and securing transactions and prevent spam by making it costly to run unnecessary operations.

Ethereum originally used a proof-of-work (PoW) consensus mechanism, similar to Bitcoin's mining process. However, in 2022, Ethereum completed "The Merge," transitioning to proof-of-stake (PoS). In PoS, validators are chosen to create new blocks and confirm transactions based on the amount of ETH they have staked as collateral. This method drastically reduces energy consumption — by over 99% — while maintaining security and decentralization.

Smart contracts are the real game-changer. A smart contract is a piece of code stored on the blockchain that executes automatically when predetermined conditions are met. For example, a smart contract could be programmed to release funds to a freelancer only after work is approved, or to transfer ownership of a digital asset the moment payment is received. Because the code is public and immutable, all parties can trust that the rules will be followed exactly as written — without lawyers, banks, or third parties involved.

One of Ethereum's most explosive growth areas is

decentralized finance (DeFi). DeFi platforms allow users to lend, borrow, earn interest, trade assets, and more — all without traditional banks. These services run entirely on smart contracts, meaning transactions settle in minutes, fees are often lower, and the system is open to anyone with an internet connection. Another major use case is NFTs, which are unique digital assets representing ownership of things like art, music, or in-game items, secured on the Ethereum blockchain.

However, Ethereum also faces challenges. High demand can lead to network congestion, causing gas fees to spike. Developers are working on scaling solutions, such as "layer 2" networks like Arbitrum and Optimism, which process transactions off-chain before settling them on the main Ethereum blockchain. Ethereum's planned upgrades aim to make the network faster, cheaper, and more energy-efficient, positioning it to handle billions of users.

For anyone entering the crypto space, understanding Ethereum is crucial because it represents the evolution of blockchain from a simple payment system to a programmable platform for innovation. Bitcoin proved that decentralized money was possible; Ethereum proved that decentralized applications were possible. This shift has already created multi-billion-dollar industries and will likely shape the future of finance, commerce, and digital ownership.

Now, lets go over Adaeze's story

In Lagos, Nigeria, Adaeze was building a small online marketplace for local artisans. Her goal was simple: help weavers, potters, and jewelry makers sell their goods to buyers worldwide. But there was a problem — payments. International transfers were expensive, slow, and often blocked due to banking restrictions. One afternoon, while researching alternatives, she stumbled upon Ethereum.

At first, Adaeze assumed it was just like Bitcoin — a digital currency to send and receive payments. But as she read more, she discovered smart contracts. The idea that she could set up an agreement between buyers and sellers that executed automatically fascinated her. She imagined a buyer in London paying for a handmade bracelet, and the smart contract releasing the payment to the artisan only once the delivery was confirmed. No bank delays, no high fees, no middleman.

Determined to try it, Adaeze hired a freelance developer to build a simple smart contract on Ethereum. The first test sale was between a customer in Canada and a basket weaver in her village. The customer paid in Ether, the smart contract held the funds, and as soon as the package was scanned by the courier for delivery, the payment was released to the artisan. It worked flawlessly. The weaver received her payment in minutes instead of weeks, and the customer was delighted by the speed and transparency.

Encouraged, Adaeze began exploring more possibilities. She learned about decentralized finance (DeFi) and realized she could allow artisans to deposit their earnings into a DeFi platform and earn interest — something unheard of in their local banking system. She also discovered NFTs and considered creating digital certificates of authenticity for every product, so buyers could verify that their handmade items were genuine.

But it wasn't all smooth sailing. One day, a spike in network activity caused gas fees to skyrocket, making small transactions impractical. Adaeze had to quickly adapt, moving part of her system to a layer 2 scaling solution to keep costs low. She also educated her artisans on how to safely store their Ether and avoid scams, knowing that personal responsibility was essential in the crypto world.

Within a year, Adaeze's platform had connected hundreds of artisans to customers in over 20 countries. Payments were faster, fees were lower, and trust was higher than ever before. For her, Ethereum was more than a technology — it was an equalizer, giving small business owners in developing nations the same global reach as big corporations.

One evening, as she watched an elderly weaver check her first Ethereum payment on a smartphone, Adaeze realized something profound: Ethereum had not only changed her business — it had changed lives. In a world where many had been excluded from the financial system, Ethereum opened the door to global opportunity, one smart contract at a time.

Chapter 6: Altcoins and How They Differ from Bitcoin and Ethereum

The term *altcoin* stands for "alternative coin," and it refers to any cryptocurrency that is not Bitcoin. When Bitcoin was first introduced in 2009, it was the only cryptocurrency in existence. But as the underlying blockchain technology became more widely understood, developers began creating new coins and tokens with their own features, purposes, and communities. Some altcoins aim to improve upon Bitcoin's design, while others target entirely different problems and industries.

Ethereum, technically, is an altcoin because it is not Bitcoin, but it has become such a dominant player that it's often discussed separately. The thousands of other altcoins vary widely in purpose, structure, and value. Some, like Litecoin, were created to offer faster transactions or lower fees compared to Bitcoin. Others, like Cardano and Polkadot, aim to build scalable platforms for smart contracts and decentralized applications. Still others, like Monero and Zcash, focus on privacy, offering transactions that are completely anonymous.

Many altcoins serve as the native currencies of specific blockchain ecosystems. For example, Binance Coin (BNB) powers transactions on the Binance Smart Chain, while Solana's SOL token is used for fees and staking on the Solana network. Some altcoins are stablecoins, such as USD Coin (USDC) or Tether (USDT), which are pegged to the value of a fiat currency to reduce volatility. Stablecoins are especially popular for trading, lending, and transferring value without worrying about price swings.

One of the biggest differences between Bitcoin and most altcoins is governance and development speed. Bitcoin's network changes very slowly due to its conservative approach to upgrades, prioritizing security and stability. Altcoins, on the other hand, often experiment with new features, consensus mechanisms, and tokenomics. This innovation can lead to significant advancements, but it also means higher risk, as some altcoins fail due to poor design, lack of adoption, or even outright fraud.

Investing in altcoins can be both rewarding and risky. While Bitcoin is considered relatively stable in the crypto world, altcoins can experience much higher volatility. It is not uncommon for smaller altcoins to rise or fall by double-digit percentages in a single day. Successful altcoin investing requires research into the project's team, technology, use case, community support, and long-term viability. Without due diligence, investors risk putting money into "pump-and-dump" schemes or tokens with no real utility.

Another important difference is market perception. Bitcoin is seen by many as "digital gold" — a store of value and hedge against inflation. Ethereum is viewed as a "world computer" powering decentralized applications. Altcoins can be seen as either high-potential innovations or speculative gambles, depending on the project. Some altcoins have real-world partnerships and active ecosystems, while others exist solely to capitalize on hype.

For new crypto users, the safest approach is to understand Bitcoin first, then Ethereum, and only then explore altcoins with caution. While altcoins have the potential for higher returns, they also carry significantly more risk. The key is to recognize that not all altcoins are created equal — and in many cases, only a small fraction will survive in the long run.

In short, altcoins represent the experimental side of the cryptocurrency market. They are where innovation happens rapidly, fortunes are made and lost quickly, and new blockchain technologies are tested. Understanding the differences between Bitcoin, Ethereum, and the thousands of altcoins is essential for making informed decisions in the crypto space.

The story of Rafael and his alternative investments

In Manila, a young software student named Rafael had been dabbling in Bitcoin for a year. It was steady and reliable, but he wanted to see if there were other opportunities in the crypto world. One evening, while scrolling through a forum, he came across a discussion about something called Solana. People were talking about its lightning-fast transactions and low fees compared to Ethereum. Curious, Rafael decided to dig deeper.

He learned that Solana was designed for speed, capable of processing thousands of transactions per second, and that its token, SOL, was used for staking and paying transaction fees. It wasn't just a currency — it was the fuel for an entire blockchain ecosystem. The more Rafael researched, the more he realized there was a whole universe of cryptocurrencies beyond Bitcoin and Ethereum.

His next discovery was Cardano, a project that prided itself on academic research and peer-reviewed development. Cardano's ADA token wasn't just about payments — it powered a platform for smart contracts with a strong focus on sustainability and scalability. Rafael admired the project's methodical approach, but he also noticed it was slower to release features compared to competitors.

One of the most surprising finds was Monero, a privacy coin that hid transaction details completely. While Bitcoin transactions were pseudonymous but still visible on the blockchain, Monero's were invisible to outsiders. This appealed to people who valued financial privacy, but it also attracted controversy from regulators. Rafael began to see that each altcoin had its own strengths, weaknesses, and political challenges.

Rafael decided to invest a small amount into several altcoins, treating it as a learning experience. Some of his picks did well, especially when a DeFi boom sent tokens like Uniswap's UNI soaring. Others lost value quickly when interest faded. He learned that hype could push prices up fast, but without strong technology and an active user base, those gains often didn't last.

Through trial and error, Rafael began developing his own strategy: research first, invest small, and take profits when prices spiked. He avoided coins that existed only because of memes or celebrity endorsements, preferring projects with clear goals and real utility. Over time, he built a small portfolio of altcoins alongside his Bitcoin and Ethereum holdings.

One night, while explaining the differences between Bitcoin, Ethereum, and altcoins to a friend, Rafael realized something important. Bitcoin had taught him the value of decentralization, Ethereum had shown him the power of smart contracts, and altcoins had opened his eyes to the endless creativity of the crypto community. He understood now that while not all altcoins would succeed, the innovations they introduced could shape the future of the entire industry.

For Rafael, altcoins weren't just risky bets — they were the testing ground for ideas that could one day change the way the world used money, technology, and trust.

Chapter 7: Stablecoins and Their Role in the Crypto Economy

Stablecoins are a unique category of cryptocurrency designed to maintain a stable value, usually pegged to a traditional currency like the U.S. dollar, the euro, or even commodities like gold. While Bitcoin and most altcoins are known for their volatility, stablecoins aim to provide price stability, making them useful for payments, savings, and trading without the risk of sudden price swings. In essence, they combine the advantages of digital currencies with the reliability of traditional money.

There are several types of stablecoins, each with its own method of maintaining stability. **Fiat-collateralized stablecoins** are backed by reserves of traditional currency held in banks or trusted institutions. For example, USD Coin (USDC) and Tether (USDT) each claim to hold one U.S. dollar in reserve for every token in circulation. When you buy one USDC, it should be redeemable for one actual U.S. dollar, making it stable as long as the issuer maintains proper reserves.

Crypto-collateralized stablecoins are backed by other cryptocurrencies instead of fiat currency. Because cryptocurrencies are volatile, these stablecoins are often overcollateralized — meaning you must deposit more value in crypto than the stablecoins you receive. A popular example is DAI, which is backed by Ethereum and other assets through the MakerDAO system. If the value of the collateral drops too much, the system automatically liquidates it to maintain the peg.

Algorithmic stablecoins don't rely on collateral at all. Instead, they use smart contracts and algorithms to adjust the supply of the coin to keep its value stable. If the price goes above the peg, the system increases supply; if it falls below, the system reduces supply. While innovative, algorithmic stablecoins can be risky, as shown by the collapse of TerraUSD (UST) in 2022, which caused billions in losses.

Stablecoins have become essential in the crypto economy for several reasons. First, they provide a safe haven for traders. Instead of cashing out to a bank account during market volatility, traders can move funds into stablecoins, avoiding the delays and fees of converting to fiat. Second, they enable global transactions without the need for traditional banking systems. A person in one country can send USDC to someone in another country instantly, with low fees, and the recipient receives a dollar-equivalent value without worrying about exchange rates.

In the world of decentralized finance (DeFi), stablecoins are the backbone of lending, borrowing, and yield farming. They serve as collateral for loans, trading pairs on decentralized exchanges, and a base currency for generating interest. For businesses, stablecoins can be used to pay suppliers, employees, or freelancers in different countries quickly and cheaply, all while maintaining price stability.

However, stablecoins are not without risks. Fiat-backed stablecoins require trust in the issuing company to actually hold the reserves they claim. Crypto-backed and algorithmic stablecoins depend on smart contract security and market stability. Regulatory scrutiny is increasing, with governments concerned about their impact on the financial system, money laundering risks, and the possibility of runs on stablecoin reserves.

For newcomers to crypto, stablecoins are often the easiest entry point because they behave like digital dollars. They allow people to interact with blockchain technology without exposing themselves to extreme volatility. Understanding stablecoins is essential because they bridge the gap between traditional finance and the fast-moving world of cryptocurrency, offering a foundation for payments, savings, and investment strategies in the digital age.

The story of Maria and the speed of crypto

In Manila, Maria ran a small online business selling handmade home décor. Most of her customers were from the United States and Europe, but getting paid was always a challenge. International bank transfers were slow and expensive, and currency exchange rates often ate into her profits. One day, a returning customer suggested paying her in USDC, a stablecoin pegged to the U.S. dollar. Maria had never heard of it before, but she was intrigued.

Her customer explained that USDC worked like a digital dollar. It could be sent over the blockchain, arriving in minutes instead of days, and without the high fees charged by banks or payment processors. Maria decided to give it a try. She downloaded a crypto wallet app, received the payment, and watched as the transaction confirmed almost instantly. The amount was exactly what her customer sent — no exchange rate losses, no hidden charges.

Encouraged, Maria started offering stablecoin payments to other customers. Soon, about half of her sales were in USDC or USDT. She discovered she could convert them to pesos on a local crypto exchange whenever she needed cash, or she could keep them in her wallet as savings without worrying about value fluctuations. For the first time, she felt she had a reliable way to handle international payments without being at the mercy of the banking system.

Maria's curiosity grew. She learned about DAI, a decentralized stablecoin backed by crypto collateral, and experimented with earning interest by depositing her USDC into a DeFi lending platform. The returns were far higher than any savings account at her bank. She even started paying some of her suppliers in stablecoins, cutting down on delays and fees for them as well.

One evening, a supplier asked why she preferred stablecoins over regular cryptocurrency like Bitcoin. Maria explained that while Bitcoin's value could rise or fall dramatically in a single day, stablecoins stayed steady, making it easier to plan her finances. "It's like having the speed of crypto without the rollercoaster ride," she said.

Over time, Maria's business grew, partly because she could serve customers in countries she had previously avoided due to payment issues. She became a local advocate for stablecoins, teaching other small business owners how to accept them safely. While she still kept an eye on regulatory developments, Maria knew stablecoins had transformed her business.

For her, they weren't just a new form of payment — they were a bridge between her small online store in the Philippines and the global marketplace, opening doors that traditional finance had kept closed for years.

Chapter 8: How to Buy, Sell, and Store Cryptocurrency Safely

Buying cryptocurrency has become much easier over the years, but doing it safely requires understanding the different options, risks, and best practices. The most common way to purchase crypto is through **cryptocurrency exchanges**, which act as marketplaces where you can trade traditional currency (fiat) for digital currency. Popular centralized exchanges include Coinbase, Binance, and Kraken. These platforms are user-friendly, often allowing you to buy crypto using a debit card, bank transfer, or even PayPal in some regions.

While centralized exchanges are convenient, they require you to trust the company with your funds and personal information. This means you are subject to their rules, withdrawal limits, and security measures. For greater control, some users prefer **decentralized exchanges (DEXs)** like Uniswap or PancakeSwap, where trades happen directly between users via smart contracts without intermediaries. DEXs offer more privacy but can be harder for beginners to navigate.

Once you buy cryptocurrency, **storage** becomes the most important consideration. Leaving funds on an exchange for long periods is risky because exchanges can be hacked or freeze accounts. Instead, many experienced users transfer their crypto to personal wallets. There are two main types of wallets: **hot wallets** and **cold wallets**.

Hot wallets are connected to the internet, such as mobile apps, desktop wallets, or browser-based wallets like MetaMask. They are convenient for frequent transactions but more vulnerable to hacking. Cold wallets, on the other hand, are offline storage devices like hardware wallets (Ledger, Trezor) or even paper wallets. Because they are not connected to the internet, cold wallets are far more secure for long-term storage.

When selling cryptocurrency, you can use the same exchanges you used to buy it, either converting it back into fiat currency or swapping it for another cryptocurrency. Peer-to-peer (P2P) marketplaces like LocalBitcoins or Binance P2P allow you to sell directly to another person, often with more payment options, but they require caution to avoid scams.

Security is a critical part of buying, selling, and storing crypto. Always enable two-factor authentication (2FA) on your accounts, avoid sharing private keys or recovery phrases, and beware of phishing scams. Never click suspicious links or respond to unsolicited messages claiming to be from an exchange or wallet provider. Keep multiple backups of your wallet recovery phrase in secure, offline locations.

Another safety tip is to start small when using a new platform or sending crypto for the first time. Send a test transaction with a small amount to confirm the wallet address before sending larger sums. Remember, crypto transactions are irreversible — once sent, they cannot be canceled or retrieved without the recipient's cooperation.

Finally, be aware of your country's regulations. Some jurisdictions require identity verification before buying or selling crypto, and profits from trading may be taxable. Keeping records of your transactions will help you stay compliant and avoid legal issues. By combining knowledge, caution, and the right tools, you can confidently buy, sell, and store cryptocurrency while protecting your assets.

Piotr story

In Warsaw, Poland, Piotr had been following cryptocurrency news for months, watching Bitcoin's price rise and fall like a tide. He wanted to buy some, but the idea of sending money to a mysterious website made him uneasy. After some research, he decided to start with a well-known exchange. He chose one with strong security reviews and a simple interface, linked his bank account, and made his first small purchase — 0.002 BTC. Seeing it appear in his account felt surreal.

At first, Piotr left his Bitcoin on the exchange, but a news story about a major hack convinced him to look into wallets. He downloaded a mobile wallet app, transferred a small amount, and was relieved to see the transfer complete in minutes. Then he read about hardware wallets and decided to invest in one for long-term storage. Holding the small device in his hand, he felt a sense of ownership he never got from his bank's online account.

A few months later, Piotr decided to sell a portion of his Bitcoin to cover some expenses. He used the same exchange to sell, converting the crypto to euros, which he withdrew to his bank account. The process was smoother than he expected, but it taught him the importance of timing — prices could change significantly even within an hour.

One day, a friend told him about a decentralized exchange. Curious, Piotr tried swapping a small amount of Ethereum for a different token directly from his wallet. There was no sign-up, no bank involved — just a direct blockchain transaction. He was amazed at the independence it offered, but also cautious, knowing that with no customer support, any mistake would be permanent.

Over time, Piotr developed strict habits. He always double-checked wallet addresses, enabled two-factor authentication, and kept his recovery phrases locked in a fireproof safe. He ignored suspicious messages and resisted offers that seemed too good to be true. These precautions kept his funds safe even when a phishing scam targeted several people in his city.

For Piotr, buying his first Bitcoin was the start of a new financial journey. But learning how to store it securely was what gave him true confidence. He knew that the crypto world could be unpredictable, but with the right tools and discipline, he could participate in it on his own terms — without leaving his security to chance.

Chapter 9: Avoiding Scams and Common Mistakes in Cryptocurrency

The cryptocurrency industry offers immense opportunities, but it is also a target-rich environment for scammers and hackers. Because transactions are irreversible and the system is decentralized, once you send your funds to a scammer, there's virtually no way to get them back. This is why learning how to recognize and avoid scams is one of the most important skills for anyone entering the crypto space.

One of the most common types of scams is the **phishing attack**. This involves tricking you into revealing your private keys, recovery phrases, or login credentials through fake websites, emails, or messages. Scammers often create realistic-looking copies of popular exchanges or wallets, sending links via social media or email that lead to these fake pages. Once you enter your details, they take control of your account. The best defense is to always type website addresses manually, bookmark official links, and never click on suspicious links.

Another prevalent scam is the **Ponzi or pyramid scheme**, where early investors are paid with funds from new investors rather than from actual profits. These schemes promise high, guaranteed returns with little or no risk. In the crypto space, they often involve new tokens or "investment platforms" that disappear once enough money has been collected. If an offer sounds too good to be true, it almost always is.

Pump-and-dump schemes are also common. Here, a group of people artificially inflates the price of a low-market-cap cryptocurrency through coordinated buying and hype on social media. Once the price spikes, they sell their holdings for a profit, causing the price to crash and leaving late buyers with heavy losses. Avoid chasing sudden, unexplained price surges and always research a project's fundamentals before investing.

Another trap for newcomers is **fake giveaways**. Scammers impersonate celebrities, influencers, or even legitimate companies, claiming that if you send them crypto, they will send you back double. These scams often use social media or hacked accounts to appear credible. Legitimate giveaways never require you to send money first.

Common mistakes also lead to losses, even without scams involved. Sending funds to the wrong wallet address is one of the biggest. Because crypto transactions are irreversible, a single character error in an address can mean your funds are lost forever. Always copy and paste wallet addresses, double-check them, and consider sending a small test transaction first.

Storing crypto on unsecured devices is another major risk. If your computer or phone is infected with malware, hackers can steal your private keys. Use reputable antivirus software, keep your system updated, and avoid downloading unverified apps. Also, never share your recovery phrase online or store it in cloud services, which can be hacked.

One of the best defenses is skepticism. In crypto, urgency is often a red flag — scammers pressure you to act quickly so you don't have time to think. Take your time, verify information, and consult trusted sources before making decisions.

Ultimately, protecting yourself in crypto requires a combination of knowledge, caution, and discipline. By understanding how scams work and avoiding common mistakes, you can focus on the legitimate opportunities that this industry offers — without becoming a statistic.

Elena's new crypto project

In Toronto, Elena had been trading crypto for just a few months when she received a direct message on social media. The sender claimed to be from a well-known exchange, offering her a special promotion: if she sent 0.1 BTC to a specific address, they would "double her holdings" as part of a limited-time loyalty program. The message looked official, complete with the exchange's logo and a signature from someone posing as a senior account manager.

At first, Elena felt excited — who wouldn't want free Bitcoin? But then she remembered an article she had read about common scams. It specifically mentioned fake giveaways and the "send crypto to get more back" trick. To be sure, she went to the official exchange website and contacted their support team. They confirmed the message was fake. By resisting the pressure to act quickly, she saved herself from losing thousands of dollars.

A few weeks later, Elena's friend Mark wasn't so lucky. He joined a new crypto project he had seen hyped on a forum. The project's team promised "guaranteed 50% monthly returns" and claimed their secret trading algorithm was risk-free. Mark invested heavily. For the first two months, he received regular payouts, which made him believe it was real. But in the third month, the website went offline, the social media accounts disappeared, and the team was nowhere to be found. It was a classic Ponzi scheme.

Determined not to repeat Mark's mistake, Elena made security her top priority. She bought a hardware wallet, enabled two-factor authentication, and only used exchanges with strong reputations. She also adopted the habit of sending small test transactions before transferring large amounts. One night, that habit saved her from disaster — she realized she had accidentally copied the wrong wallet address due to a malicious browser extension. Because she had only sent a small amount first, she avoided losing her full balance.

Elena also became cautious with hype-driven coins. She once saw a token's price skyrocket overnight after a famous influencer mentioned it. The chatrooms were full of people urging her to buy before it "went to the moon." Instead, she waited and researched. Within days, the price collapsed — it had been a pump-and-dump. Her patience kept her from joining the long list of traders left holding worthless tokens.

Over time, Elena learned that in the crypto world, trust had to be earned slowly, and anything promising quick riches was almost always a trap. She began teaching others about scam awareness, sharing real examples and practical tips. While she couldn't stop scammers from trying, she knew she could help others recognize the warning signs.

For Elena, the lesson was clear: in cryptocurrency, protecting your assets isn't just about secure storage — it's about securing your judgment. The more she learned, the more she realized that knowledge and caution were her most valuable investments.

Chapter 10: The Future of Cryptocurrency and Blockchain

The future of cryptocurrency and blockchain is both exciting and uncertain. While no one can predict exactly how the industry will evolve, the trends we see today give us strong clues about where it is headed. Cryptocurrency has already moved from a niche interest among tech enthusiasts to a global financial phenomenon, attracting individuals, institutions, and even governments. The next decade will likely bring even greater adoption, integration, and innovation.

One of the biggest trends shaping the future is **mainstream adoption**. Major corporations are beginning to accept cryptocurrency payments, and large investment firms are adding Bitcoin and Ethereum to their portfolios. Payment processors like PayPal and Visa now support crypto transactions, making it easier for consumers to use digital currencies in daily life. As more people interact with crypto, the user experience will likely become simpler, reducing the technical barriers that have kept some people away.

Regulation will also play a major role. Governments around the world are working to develop rules for cryptocurrency markets, balancing innovation with consumer protection. While some fear regulation will stifle growth, clear legal frameworks could actually boost adoption by giving institutional investors and traditional businesses the confidence to participate. In parallel, central banks are exploring **central bank digital currencies (CBDCs)**, which are government-backed digital versions of fiat currency that could coexist with decentralized cryptocurrencies.

The rise of **decentralized finance (DeFi)** is another major force shaping the future. DeFi platforms already allow users to borrow, lend, trade, and earn interest without banks. As these systems mature, they could rival traditional financial institutions in efficiency, accessibility, and global reach. Similarly, **non-fungible tokens (NFTs)** are transforming industries like art, gaming, real estate, and digital identity, creating new opportunities for ownership and monetization.

Technological innovation will drive the next wave of blockchain applications. **Scalability solutions** like layer 2 networks, sharding, and improved consensus algorithms will allow blockchains to process thousands of transactions per second at low cost. **Interoperability protocols** will connect different blockchains, enabling seamless transfers of assets and data between platforms. Advances in privacy technology will make it possible to conduct fully private yet verifiable transactions, expanding blockchain's use in sensitive industries like healthcare and finance.

One area with enormous potential is the **tokenization of real-world assets**. In the future, everything from real estate to stocks, bonds, and even intellectual property could be represented as blockchain-based tokens. This could make ownership more transparent, transactions faster, and investments more accessible to people worldwide. Imagine being able to buy a fraction of a skyscraper or a Picasso painting in seconds, all recorded securely on a blockchain.

Despite the optimism, challenges remain. Volatility, energy consumption (for proof-of-work systems), and security vulnerabilities will need to be addressed. Public perception still fluctuates between excitement and skepticism, and the industry must work to earn trust through transparency, education, and responsible development.

Ultimately, the future of cryptocurrency and blockchain will depend on how well the technology can integrate into everyday life. Just as the internet became indispensable over time, blockchain could become the invisible infrastructure behind finance, commerce, and data exchange. Whether you're an investor, developer, or everyday user, understanding and engaging with this technology now will prepare you for a world where blockchain is as common as email or credit cards.

Now, let's talk about Aaron and his story

In Singapore, Aaron sat on the balcony of his apartment, looking out over the glowing skyline. Five years earlier, he had bought his first Bitcoin out of curiosity. Now, cryptocurrency wasn't just part of his portfolio – it was part of his life. He used stablecoins to pay freelancers in other countries, earned interest through DeFi platforms, and even owned fractional shares of real estate through blockchain-based tokens.

Aaron's favorite project was a decentralized marketplace for digital art, where he had purchased several NFTs. At first, his friends laughed at the idea of "buying a picture you can't hang on the wall," but they stopped laughing when one of his pieces tripled in value. He explained that NFTs were more than art – they were proof of ownership in a digital world, and they could represent anything from music rights to virtual land.

One day, Aaron's company received an invitation to pilot a new government program using blockchain for international trade. The system tokenized shipping documents, eliminating weeks of paperwork and reducing fraud. Transactions that once required multiple banks, lawyers, and customs agencies now settled instantly on a secure, shared ledger. The savings in time and cost were staggering.

Aaron also watched as his parents, once skeptical of crypto, began using a central bank digital currency to pay bills and shop online. They didn't care about blockchain's technical details — they just liked that it was fast, cheap, and easy. Aaron realized that mass adoption might not come from people seeking decentralization or financial freedom, but from everyday conveniences that made life better.

Still, he knew the industry had growing pains ahead. A friend had recently lost money in a poorly secured DeFi project, and scams continued to target newcomers. But Aaron believed these issues would fade as regulation, security standards, and education improved. Just as the early internet had its share of fraud and chaos, blockchain would mature and stabilize over time.

One night, Aaron met a young developer at a networking event. She spoke passionately about creating a blockchain platform that connected renewable energy producers with consumers directly, allowing households to buy clean energy in real time. Listening to her, Aaron felt the same spark of excitement he had when he first learned about Bitcoin. He saw a future where blockchain wasn't just about trading tokens but about solving real-world problems at scale.

As the city lights reflected off the harbor, Aaron thought about how far crypto had come – and how much further it could go. He knew there would be setbacks, but he also knew one thing for certain: blockchain was here to stay. The only question was who would be ready to seize the opportunities it created.

Chapter 11: Cryptocurrency Taxes and Legal Considerations

As cryptocurrency adoption grows, governments around the world are establishing tax rules and legal frameworks for digital assets. For anyone involved in buying, selling, or earning cryptocurrency, understanding tax obligations is essential to avoid legal trouble and unexpected bills. While the specific laws vary by country, most tax authorities treat cryptocurrency as property or a capital asset, meaning transactions can trigger taxable events.

In many countries, **capital gains tax** applies when you sell cryptocurrency for fiat currency, trade one cryptocurrency for another, or use crypto to purchase goods or services. The gain or loss is calculated by subtracting the purchase price (cost basis) from the sale price. If you held the crypto for more than a year before selling, you may qualify for a lower long-term capital gains tax rate; if you held it for less than a year, short-term rates — often the same as regular income tax — apply.

Income tax may also apply if you receive cryptocurrency as payment for goods or services, through mining rewards, staking, or airdrops. In these cases, the fair market value of the crypto at the time you receive it is counted as income, and you may owe tax on that amount even if you don't sell it immediately. This can create a challenge if the crypto's value drops later, as the tax is still based on its value at the time you received it.

Some jurisdictions require **detailed record-keeping** for every crypto transaction, including dates, amounts, wallet addresses, and the fiat value at the time of each transaction. Crypto tax software can automate much of this tracking by integrating with your wallets and exchanges, generating tax reports that comply with local laws.

On the legal side, regulations vary widely. Some countries, like El Salvador, have embraced cryptocurrency as legal tender, while others have banned it outright. Many nations fall somewhere in between, allowing crypto trading but imposing strict rules on exchanges and requiring compliance with **know-your-customer (KYC)** and **anti-money-laundering (AML)** regulations. These rules aim to prevent illegal activities but can affect user privacy and access.

A growing area of regulation is **reporting requirements**. Some governments now require taxpayers to declare whether they own or have traded cryptocurrency, even if no taxable event occurred. In the United States, the IRS asks about virtual currency activity on tax forms, and noncompliance can lead to penalties.

Tax laws and regulations will continue evolving as cryptocurrency becomes more integrated into the financial system. The safest approach is to stay informed, keep accurate records, and consult a tax professional who understands digital assets. By doing so, you can enjoy the benefits of cryptocurrency while staying fully compliant with the law.

Liam's crypto tax software story

In Sydney, Liam had been trading cryptocurrency for two years. He loved the excitement of the market and the sense of independence it gave him. But tax season brought a rude awakening. He received a letter from the Australian Tax Office (ATO) asking for records of his crypto trades. At first, he panicked — he had made dozens of trades across multiple exchanges and had never kept detailed records.

Determined to fix the situation, Liam started digging through his exchange histories, wallet transactions, and bank statements. It was overwhelming, but he soon discovered a crypto tax software that could import his data automatically. The software generated a report showing his capital gains and income from staking rewards. While the final tax bill wasn't small, he was relieved to have everything organized and compliant.

The experience changed Liam's habits. He began keeping detailed records of every trade, noting the date, the amount, and the fiat value at the time. He also learned the importance of setting aside money for taxes instead of reinvesting everything into new trades. A friend who failed to do this ended up selling crypto at a loss just to pay a tax bill — a mistake Liam was determined to avoid.

Liam also became more aware of the legal landscape. When one of his favorite exchanges announced it was closing to Australian customers due to regulatory changes, he realized how quickly laws could affect access. He began diversifying his holdings across different wallets and exchanges, making sure he could still access his assets if one platform shut down.

One evening, over dinner, Liam's cousin asked whether he thought taxes would ruin the benefits of crypto. Liam shook his head. "Taxes are just part of life," he said. "If anything, they mean crypto is being taken seriously now. The key is to play by the rules so you can keep playing at all."

For Liam, the lesson was simple: in the crypto world, you can't ignore the taxman or the law. But with good records and a proactive approach, you can keep your freedom – and your profits – intact.

Chapter 12: Building a Long-Term Cryptocurrency Investment Strategy

Many newcomers to cryptocurrency are drawn in by stories of quick profits, but long-term success in the space requires a clear investment strategy. Without a plan, emotional decisions and market hype can lead to costly mistakes. A long-term strategy focuses on steady growth, risk management, and patience, allowing investors to weather volatility and take advantage of emerging opportunities.

The first step is **defining your goals**. Are you looking to grow wealth over decades, generate passive income, or diversify your portfolio? Your goals will determine your approach. For long-term investors, a common strategy is **buy and hold** – purchasing quality cryptocurrencies and holding them for years, regardless of short-term price fluctuations. This approach relies on the belief that strong projects will appreciate over time as adoption grows.

Diversification is another key principle. While Bitcoin and Ethereum are considered the foundation of many portfolios, adding a selection of carefully researched altcoins can provide exposure to different sectors of the crypto market, such as DeFi, NFTs, or blockchain infrastructure. However, diversification should be balanced – holding too many low-quality altcoins can dilute returns and increase risk.

Risk management is critical. Only invest what you can afford to lose, and avoid putting all your funds into a single asset. Many investors allocate a fixed percentage of their portfolio to crypto, keeping the rest in traditional assets like stocks, bonds, or real estate. This reduces exposure to crypto's volatility while still allowing for growth.

Another strategy is **dollar-cost averaging (DCA)** – investing a fixed amount at regular intervals regardless of the asset's price. This removes the pressure of timing the market and can smooth out the effects of volatility over time. DCA works especially well for assets like Bitcoin and Ethereum, which have shown long-term growth despite short-term dips.

Long-term investors should also plan for **secure storage**. Hardware wallets are essential for protecting large holdings, and backup recovery phrases should be stored safely offline. Security breaches can undo years of gains in seconds.

Finally, staying informed is essential. The crypto landscape changes rapidly, with new technologies, regulations, and market trends emerging constantly. Regularly reviewing your portfolio, reassessing your goals, and adapting to new information will help you stay ahead.

A well-planned long-term strategy not only increases your chances of financial success but also reduces stress. Instead of reacting to every price swing, you can focus on the bigger picture, knowing your investments are aligned with your goals.

How Naledi learned to diversify her investments

In Cape Town, Naledi had watched friends jump into crypto during a bull market, only to panic-sell when prices fell. She didn't want to repeat their mistakes, so before investing a single rand, she spent months learning. She read about Bitcoin's history, Ethereum's smart contracts, and the importance of secure storage. By the time she was ready to invest, she had a plan.

Naledi decided her goal was long-term wealth building. She allocated 10% of her overall investment portfolio to cryptocurrency, focusing 70% of that on Bitcoin, 20% on Ethereum, and 10% on carefully chosen altcoins. She set up an automatic monthly purchase through an exchange, using dollar-cost averaging to build her holdings gradually. When prices dipped, she felt no panic — she saw it as an opportunity to buy at a discount.

She also invested in a hardware wallet and stored her recovery phrases in two separate, secure locations. Friends teased her about being "paranoid," but Naledi knew that in crypto, security was non-negotiable. She had heard too many stories of people losing fortunes to hacks or lost passwords.

Every three months, Naledi reviewed her portfolio. Sometimes she adjusted her altcoin holdings based on market trends, but she never strayed far from her core allocation. She ignored hype-driven projects and avoided chasing quick profits. When a co-worker tried to convince her to put half her savings into a new meme coin, she politely declined, sticking to her plan.

Years later, Naledi's patience paid off. While some of her altcoins had failed, her Bitcoin and Ethereum holdings had grown significantly in value. More importantly, she had avoided the stress and sleepless nights that came from trying to time the market. She realized her greatest advantage wasn't luck — it was discipline.

For Naledi, cryptocurrency wasn't a gamble; it was a carefully managed part of her financial future. Her strategy gave her confidence, stability, and the ability to focus on life beyond market charts. She knew the journey was far from over, but she was ready for whatever came next.

Epilogue: Your Journey Into the World of Cryptocurrency

Cryptocurrency is not just a new form of money – it's a new way of thinking about value, trust, and freedom in the digital age. As you've journeyed through this book, you've learned what cryptocurrency is, how blockchain works, the differences between major players like Bitcoin and Ethereum, the role of altcoins and stablecoins, and the essential steps for buying, storing, and protecting your assets. You've also seen the risks – from scams to regulatory changes – and discovered strategies for long-term success. The final takeaway is simple but powerful: knowledge, preparation, and discipline are your greatest allies in the crypto space.

The crypto journey is different for everyone. Some people enter the market to protect themselves against inflation, others to explore cutting-edge technology, and some simply to try a new form of investment. Whatever your reason, the principles you've learned here will serve as a compass. The crypto landscape will continue to evolve rapidly – new technologies, regulations, and market cycles will come and go – but the foundational skills you've gained will remain valuable no matter what changes.

One of the most important lessons to carry forward is the

balance between **opportunity and risk**. Cryptocurrency offers unmatched access to global finance, the ability to send value instantly across borders, and the potential for high returns. But it also demands personal responsibility. In the traditional financial system, banks, payment processors, and insurance providers can often reverse mistakes or absorb losses. In crypto, you are the custodian of your own wealth. Losing your private keys or falling for a scam can mean permanent loss. That's why secure storage, cautious investing, and skepticism toward "too good to be true" offers will always be critical.

Another key takeaway is the importance of **staying informed**. This is not an industry where you can "set it and forget it" forever. New blockchain projects are launched daily, governments are drafting new laws, and technologies like decentralized finance, NFTs, and Web3 are creating fresh opportunities and challenges. Staying connected to reliable news sources, engaging in crypto communities, and continuing to learn will help you adapt and thrive.

Equally important is remembering that crypto is about more than money. At its heart, blockchain technology is about decentralization — giving individuals the power to control their assets, their data, and in some cases, their identity. It's about creating systems where trust is placed in code and transparency, not in a single institution. This philosophy has the potential to reshape industries far beyond finance, from supply chains to voting systems, healthcare, and beyond.

As you step forward from here, consider your personal strategy. Will you be a long-term holder of Bitcoin and Ethereum, a cautious explorer of altcoins, or a hands-on participant in DeFi and NFTs? Will you use stablecoins for everyday transactions or focus solely on investments? Whatever path you choose, let it align with your goals, your risk tolerance, and your values.

Finally, remember that the crypto journey is not about chasing every market high — it's about building sustainable habits and making informed choices. Markets will rise and fall. Projects will come and go. But those who focus on fundamentals, security, and education will be in the best position to benefit from the opportunities ahead.

The future of cryptocurrency and blockchain is still being written, and you have the chance to be part of it. Whether you invest, build, trade, or simply learn, you are participating in one of the most transformative shifts in modern history. Take what you've learned, apply it wisely, and step confidently into the digital economy.

Your journey has just begun — and in the world of cryptocurrency, the possibilities are as limitless as the technology itself.

www.ingramcontent.com/pod-product-compliance
Lightning Source LLC
LaVergne TN
LVHW022022200926
848481LV00007B/2488